The Sacred Art of Listening

The Sacred Art of Listening

Forty reflections for cultivating a spiritual practice

Kay Lindahl
Founder of the Listening Center

Illustrations by **Amy Schnapper**

WILD GOOSE PUBLICATIONS
www.ionabooks.com

The Sacred Art of Listening:
Forty Reflections for Cultivating a Spiritual Practice

Text © 2002 by Kay Lindahl
Illustrations © 2002 by Amy Schnapper

Original edition published in the United States
by SkyLight Paths Publishing, Woodstock, VT, USA
www.skylightpaths.com

UK edition first published 2002 by
Wild Goose Publications
Fourth Floor, Savoy House,
140 Sauchiehall Street, Glasgow G2 3DH, UK,
the publishing division of the Iona Community.
Scottish Charity No. SCO03794.
Limited Company Reg. No. SCO96243.
www.ionabooks.com

ISBN 1 901557 65 0

Produced by Reliance Production Company, Hong Kong.
Printed and bound in China.

*This book is dedicated
to the flow of Spirit
through all forms of art
and to the possibility
of Listening
as a key to peace
in the world.*

CONTENTS

Part One: The Beginning

Part Two: Practising the Sacred Art of Listening

Contents

Contents

CONTENTS

Part Three: In Closing

Part One

THE BEGINNING

YOUR INVITATION

My own first experiences with deep listening came about through the Alliance for Spiritual Community, a grassroots interfaith organisation that I founded to promote mutual understanding and respect among people of diverse religious and cultural backgrounds. I learned that the key to reaching these goals was to create a space where we could practise the art of dialogue. After almost a decade of facilitating dialogue groups, I realised that the art of listening was the main skill that was missing for most participants. From that very real need I developed The Listening Center in California five years ago, at a time in my life when the connection between listening and the circle of life became clear to me in all its sacredness.

The Listening Center creates a place where people learn the sacred art that is listening. We lead workshops, retreats and classes around the world in our efforts to provide men and women with an experience of the value and importance of deep listening. Each person becomes a centre for listening in his or her life. Deep listening cultivates a spiritual practice. This book engages you in this process.

You are invited to use *The Sacred Art of Listening* to create more peace, harmony and love in your life and in the world. The pace of life today leaves little room for reflection and listening. The promise of this book is that you can learn to listen from the essence of your being by taking a few minutes a day for quiet time with your authentic self.

The thoughts and practices that follow are designed to expand your awareness and broaden your concept of listening. You will notice that listening as a sacred art calls forth your being in new ways. One of the greatest gifts we can give each other is the gift of our undivided attention – being present. It takes time to slow down the conversation, to include silence and reflection as well as speaking and listening.

To receive the most benefit from these teachings, I recommend using the guidelines below. They will help provide a format for you to establish a routine as you read each of the forty short chapters:

- Settle down in a quiet space.
- Slowly read one reflection.
- Gaze at the circle illustration for that reflection for a few minutes.
- Allow your mind to consider what you see and read from different perspectives.
- Notice where your heart leads you.
- Stay in the silence for a few minutes.
- Create a specific intention for improving your listening practice.
- Express gratitude for your experience.

The circle illustrations that Amy Schnapper created for *The Sacred Art of Listening* are designed to help you see the deep wisdom that lies within your own heart. There is no right or wrong way to look at the art. Rather, it is intended to engage you visually while you look into your own heart. Allow the art, the words and the teaching to move slowly into your heart while you discover levels of spirit and connection you may never have accessed before.

These reflections will introduce you to listening beyond words. The subtitle for each reflection is the practice at work. Each provides you with an opportunity to think about listening in a new way. Notice the many layers of deep listening. For example, the title of the first reflection is 'Qualities of Deep Listening'. The subtitle, or practice, is 'Listening for essence'. The desired result of this practice is to make time each day to reflect on what it is to listen for essence and to practise doing it. You will soon experience that listening is far more than hearing words.

Listening as a sacred art encompasses reflection, illustration, meditation and practice. Observe which practices in these forty reflections speak the most directly to you. Take on some of those practices. Incorporate them into your daily life. Journal your experiences in the pages at the back of this book. Be prepared for miracles.

My prayer is that just a few minutes meditating with each reflection will lead you to a deeper relationship with your Source, with your soul, and with others.

THE CIRCLE OF LIFE

The origin of *The Sacred Art of Listening* came out of a series of connected personal experiences. About five years ago, I was jolted into looking carefully at the choices I make about how I live my life. That year, on the third of May, my elder son and his wife had their first baby – a boy. What a joy it was to welcome Ryan into our family! While we were still in the glow of celebrating this new life, my mother was completing her life journey. We had a big party for her ninetieth birthday, two weeks before Ryan's birth. The gathering had been a joyous time, sharing memories of what life had been like for her, coming to this country as a young teenager. As we were all about to leave, she stood up and said, 'There is something I would like to say.' This was highly unusual. Not one to make speeches, she had always left that to my dad.

We all stopped and sat down to listen. Mother said, 'I want to thank you all for coming. It's been a lovely party and I'll see you on the other side.' We were stunned. Did she realise what she was saying, we wondered. And now we know – yes, she did. Ten days later she was admitted to the hospital, and she died on May 11. Her great-grandson Ryan was just eight days old.

Mother had become restless after a few days in the hospital. One day, she looked as though she wanted to get out of bed. 'What do you want, Mum?' I asked.

'I need to get to the door,' she said.

'What door?' I asked.

'The one over there.' She pointed over my shoulder at a blank wall. I was puzzled; she finally said, 'This isn't making any sense, is it?'

'Not a whole lot,' I replied. 'But you know, I think it will make all the sense in the world when you see what's on the other side of that door.'

The cycle of life had never been more present for me. It's one thing to know that as human beings we are born, we live for a time, and then we die − and it's another to experience personally the beginning and end of life's cycle at virtually the same moment. The synchronicity of these birth and death events caused me to reflect deeply about my own life.

How often do we find ourselves saying, 'Where has the time gone? My, how time flies. The older I get, the less time I seem to have. How quickly the days (weeks, months, years) pass by.' Suddenly, this notion of time took on a whole new dimension for me. I began to see time not as a straight line from birth to death but as a circle in which we each have a role − but just for a moment. None of us knows how much time we have to live this life, or what part of the circle we are about to experience. But to be fully alive is to be present to life each moment. Like many people, I all too easily get caught living life in the past, the 'I should haves' − or in the future, the 'someday I wills'. And yet the only time we actually have, the only time we really experience, is the present.

The birth of my grandson and the death of my mother within days of each other made me aware of the value of simply being present. I spent a lot of time being with my mother in her final days. We didn't say much. Yet something wonderful happened in those moments. I wasn't thinking about the past or the future, only about the experience of 'now' and how precious life was in those moments.

The reflections in this book all relate to time – to being present. They also relate to the circle of life in the context of the sacred art of listening. They are reflections from my journey and experiences I have had as I flow along the circle of life. They express my intention to listen deeply and completely, and to be fully present in the world around me. I hope they serve you in your journey.

We must learn to listen if there is to be peace in the world, particularly among religious traditions. Affirming the sacred art of listening is my response to this call for peace. Learning how to listen to and speak with each other are essential skills for creating relationships that lead to mutual respect, dialogue, understanding and peace. As I explore a spiritual approach to listening, my understanding of what it actually means to listen continues to expand. Listening encompasses much more than words. Listening is a way of being in the world. These reflections speak from that voice.

Part Two

PRACTISING THE SACRED ART OF LISTENING

1

QUALITIES OF DEEP LISTENING
Listening for essence

Perhaps one of the most precious and powerful gifts we can give another person is to really listen to them, to listen with quiet, fascinated attention, with our whole being, fully present. This sounds simple, but if we are honest with ourselves, we do not often listen to each other so completely.

Listening is a creative force. Something quite wonderful occurs when we are listened to fully. We expand, ideas come to life and grow, we remember who we are. Some speak of this force as a creative fountain within us that springs forth; others call it the inner spirit, intelligence, true self. Whatever this force is called, it shrivels up when we are not listened to and it thrives when we are.

The way we listen can actually allow the other person to bring forth what is true and alive to them. Sometimes we have to do a lot of listening before the fountain is replenished. Have you ever noticed how some people seem to need to talk? They go on and on, usually in a very superficial, nervous manner. This is often because they have not been truly listened to. Patience is required to listen to such a person long enough for them to get to their centre point of tranquillity and peace. The results of such listening are extraordinary. Some would call them miracles.

Listening well takes time, skill, and a readiness to slow down, to let go of expectations, judgements, boredom, self-assertiveness, defensiveness. I've noticed that when people experience the depth of being listened to like this, they also begin to listen to others in the same way.

Listening is an art that calls for practice. Imagine if we all spent just a few minutes each day practising the art of listening, being fully present with the person we are with. There would be a collective sigh of contentment and joy. Listen!

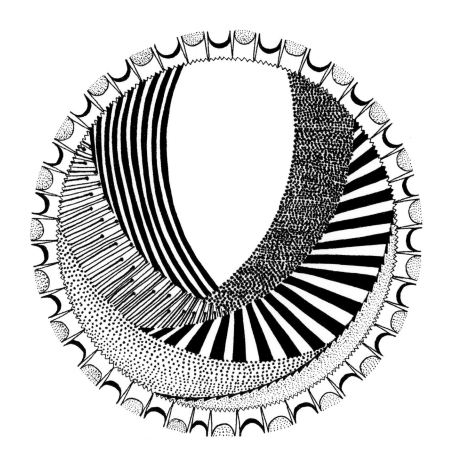

Listening is a creative force
that teaches patience.

2

Listening as spiritual awareness

Effective listening is often conceived of in technical terms that have little or no grounding in what is spiritual. There are also a lot of wonderful tools and techniques to assist us, however, such as active listening, empathic listening, responsible listening, body language, eye contact techniques, and methods identifying different styles of listening and speaking. These focus on the mechanics of listening and provide us with very useful skills and information.

The premise of my work, and the work of The Listening Center, is that listening is a sacred act. There's something beyond technique when two or more people are deeply listening to each other. It is an awareness that not only are we present to each other, we are present to something that is spiritual, holy, sacred.

We tap into the holiness of deep listening.

Over the years I have discovered that there is a basic context that nurtures and develops the practice of listening as a sacred art. Three qualities that are essential to this deep listening context are silence, reflection and presence.

- **Silence** creates the space for listening to God. It provides time to explore our relationship to Source. The practice of being in this silence nurtures our capacity to listen to others.
- **Reflection** gives us access to listening for our inner voice. The practice of taking a few breaths before responding to a situation, question or comment gives time for your true wisdom to reveal itself. It's a slowing down, waiting, practising patience.
- **Presence** is the awareness of listening to another, of connecting at the heart level. The practice of taking a mundane, ordinary activity and giving it your full attention, for example washing your hands or brushing your teeth, trains your concentration and your ability to be in the present moment with another.

These three qualities of deep listening work together in an organic process that creates the context for the art of listening. Practising them for just a few minutes a day will enhance your awareness and transform your relationships with Source, self and others.

3

USING SILENCE
Listening to access your stillpoint

Have you ever noticed the discomfort with silence in our culture? Think about the last time someone called for a moment of silence in a public gathering. The first ten to fifteen seconds are usually comfortable. After that, people tend to get restless and cough, rustle paper, cross and uncross their legs, clear their throats.

Notice what happens in daily conversation. It's as though there is an unwritten rule that whenever there's a hint of silence, someone must fill the vacuum with a rush of words. We start to talk faster and faster. Listening quickly takes a back seat to talking.

The power of silence gives us breathing room. There is wisdom in the silence. It can alter our perceptions and ability to see what is happening. It can give clarity in the midst of apparent chaos. One way to practise silence is to get centred within yourself. Take a few deep breaths before speaking. Ask what wants to be said next.

Another practice is to turn off the car radio, CD or tapes and drive in the silence. See what it's like to be centred in the midst of traffic.

One thing you might begin to notice with these practices is all of the background noises that permeate our lives. After a while you will learn to simply let them be and enjoy your own interior silence.

The power of silence is the power to slow things down, to give us a chance to reflect on what is happening, to listen to the collective wisdom, and to be present.

We are used to being present in our heads, our minds, our intellect, so the innermost self may take a while to surface. Take the time. Being present in our hearts leads to compassion, love and service. Imagine listening to silence as a global behaviour!

The innermost self may take a while to surface.

4

LEARNING FROM EXPERIENCE
Listening for new possibilities

Have you ever noticed that there are times when life feels as if it has sped up? I think of waves rolling onto the shore. As soon as one is finished, the next one comes along. Sometimes the details of daily life show up like that. Before we know it, only the milestone sort of events in life – graduations and weddings, births and deaths – mark our life's journey.

All too often, we just brace ourselves for the next wave, rather than enjoy or be present with the one just passing by. We believe we have too much to do to take the time to reflect on the day or the event. How will we ever get it all done? And yet, by allowing ourselves to integrate our experience, there's more space for new possibilities. We feel alive and have energy. We're ready for the next wave and actually look forward to seeing how it builds and crests and tumbles.

Listen from your experience to discover new possibilities.

Reflection can teach us to be better listeners – to ourselves, to God and to others. Wisdom tells me there's something very important about taking time to acknowledge what happens each day. This is a part of my listening practice. It can take the form of a journal, a walk on the beach, a conversation with a close friend, or some quiet time with myself.

I've learned to ask myself questions in order to become a more reflective listener to myself and others. Try asking these questions in your own practice:

- What just happened?
- What did I learn from that?
- How did I grow from that?
- What's next for me?
- How did this impact others in my life?
- How does it relate to patterns in my past?
- What learning can I share with others?

Taking the time to explore these questions opens us up to the creative possibilities in listening. The key is to give ourselves permission to 'do nothing' – to value our experience enough to honour it with silence, to daydream without feeling guilty. When we do, we will approach our listening with others renewed, refreshed, and with a sense of awe and wonder. New possibilities will show themselves when we listen this way.

5

COMMUNION
Listening to communicate

'This is the information age' is a common mantra these days. It leads us to want to know everything and to know it right now. We are inundated with data.

The world has moved from typewriters and one carbon copy, to electric typewriters and multiple carbon copies, to copy machines and word processors, to fax machines, to e-mail, laptops, PalmPilots and broadband – all in a relatively short period of time. Add pagers, voice mail and mobile phones to the input from television, radio and newspapers and suddenly we find ourselves on the receiving end of massive amounts of data twenty-four hours a day.

Interestingly, much of this occurs without any personal interaction. Sometimes I do most of my communicating without talking directly to another human being.

Then there are days of back-to-back meetings and appointments when all I do is talk to other people. I share information and exchange data at a rapid pace. There's hardly a moment to take a breath.

All this can leave me with a yearning, a feeling that something is missing in all of this communication. We've become experts at imparting information, communicating from our heads. What's missing is connection – communicating from our hearts.

Heart communication happens when we slow down, when we quiet down, look and listen. Stop to take a breath. Become fully present with the person we're with. Listen with all of our being. At this point, communication can occur without words. Being present is a gift that fills our hearts and spirits. We are in communion.

Imagine a world where we all communicate from our hearts every day. Heart communication could be as simple as a smile or giving undivided attention to another. What a gift!

Communication can happen without words.

6

RITUALS
Listening for meaning

Rituals provide us with ways to acknowledge or remind us of something important. When many of us hear the word 'ritual', we think only of religious services. Yet, I expect that most of us have a morning ritual, whether it's reading the paper, grabbing a cup of coffee, or brushing our teeth! They are repeated patterns of meaningful acts – they help us to set the tone for our days.

I use two rituals to set the context for my work in the sacred art of listening. These two rituals transform the ordinary into something special and create a safe and sacred space by acknowledging the presence of spirit in daily life and in our work together.

The first ritual is to light a candle, which is a symbol for light, Spirit, Creator, Source, life. Lighting the candle is a ritual that acknowledges

Create an environment that calls
for listening in a new way.

the sacred right here and now. The candle also becomes a reminder to look for light in each other throughout our time together.

One participant in a Listening Center workshop took this idea home with her and began to light a candle whenever she wanted to have an important conversation with her teenage daughter. She used the ritual only occasionally, and it seemed to help them through some difficult times.

One day she was rushing around getting ready to leave for an important meeting. Her daughter came up to her and said, 'Mum, do you have a minute to talk?' She was just about to put her daughter off until later when, out of the corner of her eye, she noticed that the candle was lit. Needless to say, she stayed to listen to her daughter.

The second ritual is based on people sitting in a circle, which is fundamental for listening in groups. The ritual is to walk around the circle. As I walk, I invite participants to draw the circle with me by tracing the circle with their eyes and looking at each person as if seeing him or her for the first time. I ask them to silently acknowledge, welcome and appreciate each other. The circle then becomes the symbol of sacred space as we learn the art of listening. The ritual of circle draws the boundary between social time and sacred time. We connect.

Rituals create an environment that calls for listening in a new way as we begin our exploration of what it is to take on listening as a spiritual practice. Create your own rituals to add to your spiritual practice.

7

DIALOGUE OR DISCUSSION
Listening for context

Words, words, words, words. When we talk with each other, you may think we are having a discussion, when what I expected was a dialogue.

Dialogue comes from the Greek *dia,* which means 'through,' combined with *logos.* Dialogue literally means words flowing through. In a flow of conversation, new understandings emerge that might not have been present otherwise. Dialogue, conducted in a spirit of enquiry and a genuine desire to understand, is an open-ended exploration.

Discussion comes from the Latin *dis,* which means 'apart,' and *quatere,* 'to shake'. Discussion has the same root as percussion and concussion, meaning to break things up. In a conversation each person is analysing the subject, looking for answers, results or agreement.

There is another way to distinguish these words. Discussion leads from the intellect. Dialogue leads from the heart. Each can certainly be based on either heart or intellect, but the overall context is different. One is not better than the other – both are valid means of communicating. It's simply useful to know where you are.

Most of the time we dance back and forth between discussion and dialogue. We make no distinction, which often leads to misunderstandings. If I think we are having an open-ended exploration and you think we are going to resolve a problem, we are really in two different kinds of conversations. Distinguishing which type of conversation we are having leads to greater understanding.

There are also topics that seem to be nondiscussable. No one mentions them – they are just there, underneath the surface, blocking deep heart-to-heart communication. The dialogue process provides a safe space for these conversations.

We live in a world that blurs the lines between dialogue and discussion. Having some dialogue guidelines to follow creates an atmosphere where we can practice. The art of dialogue may make the difference between a world of war and a world of peace.

Notice the goal of your conversation.

8

SEEKING COMMON GROUND
Listening to appreciate

Have you ever been in a situation with someone where you felt misunderstood? Where you felt sure that no matter what you did or said, you wouldn't be appreciated? In these situations, the possibility of finding common ground is elusive. It is easy to begin to think that you must be living in different worlds.

When I am faced with this scenario, I all too easily start complaining about the other person. If only they would do such and such (usually that means doing it my way), then everything would be fine. But this kind of thinking focuses only on what is not working and contributes to a downward spiral in the relationship.

When I am able to notice that I'm behaving this way, I find I am better served by acknowledging that perhaps what is happening is

When I appreciate others I am at peace.

meant to teach me something. I pray – giving thanks for the lessons being learned and for guidance on how to understand them. This helps, yet I'm often left with the feeling that something is still missing. I have forgotten an important step in authentic listening – appreciation.

Recently I heard about a culture that has no crime. When someone does something disruptive to others, the whole village gathers in a circle. The offending person sits in the centre, and each person in turn shares what they appreciate about him or her, their good deeds, their personal qualities. Then everyone goes back to work. Nothing more is said about the disruptive behaviour. The result is a culture without crime.

The image spoke to me. I decided to use a similar approach with someone in a situation that was troubling me. First I made a list of all the things I authentically appreciated about her. Then I called and shared my list with her, with no expectation about any particular out-come. We still don't see eye to eye, and yet something has shifted in our relationship. Now, instead of complaining, I find myself focusing on what I appreciate about her. I am more at peace.

9

Listening for connection

Interfaith gatherings have taught me to respect the diverse ways we express our relationship to Source and have given me a sense of awed wonder in the presence of how much we all have in common. In our various religious and spiritual traditions we tend to talk in similar ways:

Baha'i – Lay not on any soul a load that you would not wish to be laid upon you and desire not for anyone the things you would not desire for yourself.

Buddhism – Hurt not others in ways that you yourself would find hurtful.

Christianity – Do unto others as you would have others do unto you.

Confucianism – Do not do unto others what you do not want others to do unto you.

Hinduism – Do not to others that which if done to you would cause you pain.

Islam – None of you truly have the faith if you do not desire for your brother that which you desire for yourself.

Jainism – In happiness and suffering, in joy and grief, we should regard all creatures as we regard our own self.

Judaism – What is hateful to you, do not do to your neighbour. This is the whole Torah; all the rest is commentary.

Native American – Respect for all life is the foundation.

Sikhism – Don't create enmity with anyone as God is within every one.

Wicca – If it harm none, do what you will.

Zoroastrianism – Do not do unto others all that which is not well for oneself.

In any conversation, what the speakers have in common is more powerful than what divides them. Sometimes this reality is hard to see, as so much energy and emotion can swirl around what separates us.

Imagine a world where everyone lived by these principles from the world's religious traditions. What would it take? Faith, love and trust – all are essential in creating relationships. Can I become a friend with someone not like me? Can I listen intently enough to find the centre that unites us?

Let's listen for what connects us, while appreciating that which differentiates us. This is practising the sacred art.

Take this attitude of oneness with you into the world. Give blessings, share joy, live in gratitude.

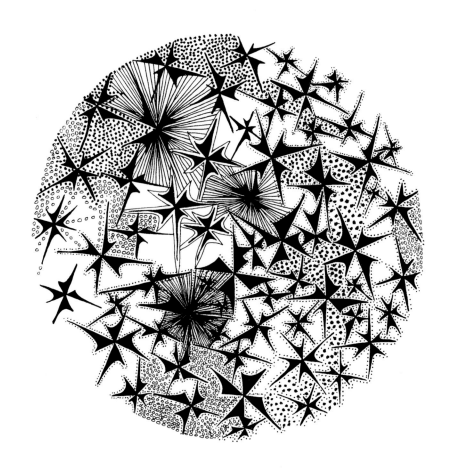

Give blessings, share joy, live in gratitude.

10

Listening from your heart

> *Yesterday is history*
> *Tomorrow is a mystery*
> *Today is a gift.*
> *That is why we call it the present.*
> —Author Unknown

One of the foundations of spiritual community is relationship. How do we relate to each other, especially to those who are not like us? By sacred listening, we can learn to be more present with each other.

Two aspects of being present in a conversation are listening and speaking. Many people are familiar with guidelines to conscious listening such as suspending assumptions and judgements and listening to understand rather than to agree or believe.

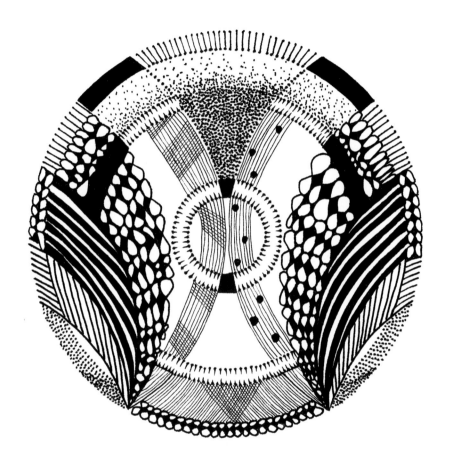

*Speaking from the 'I,' the true self, the soul,
is speaking from the heart.*

Another guideline for being truly present in our relationships is to speak from personal experience and to use 'I' language. In our culture this is an amazing challenge. Too often the subject of our conversations are 'you', 'we', 'everyone' or 'they'. This amounts to speaking from the head or the intellect, and sounds a lot like a lecture.

Speaking from the 'I', the true self, the soul, is speaking from the heart. 'I' language implies being accountable for what is said. It requires reflection to get to that place. It is the kind of speaking that connects us. Practise this and notice how it connects you to others.

Listen to the difference between these two ways of speaking. 'You know how it is when you're feeling down and you want some support and inspiration and you just can't seem to get yourself motivated.' Now listen to the true self in the present: 'I know when I'm feeling down and I want some support and inspiration and I just can't seem to get myself motivated, I feel really lonely.'

Notice the use of pronouns in conversations. In your own speaking, be a listening presence.

11

Conversations of the Heart
Listening for soul

'Heart listening' is the spiritual practice of listening from the heart and listening to the heart. Being truly listened to is one of the greatest gifts we can give each other. Heart listening is more than simply not interrupting others when they are speaking or not finishing their sentences for them. It calls upon many of the skills that we have already discerned: patience, silence, presence and appreciation. Heart listening may sound a lot like a meditation practice – it incorporates many of the same principles. Listening from the heart is being open and waiting for the other to speak what is really in their heart. As you practise, you will learn to be a heart listener and to know when you are hearing words from the heart.

Listening from the heart allows for silence and reflection. Conversation slows down and there is time to relax and feel a sense of peace. An actual sacred space is created between two people when we heart listen.

Listening to the heart also is part of this holy work. We become present to the other in such a way that they feel safe to speak what's in their heart. We practise having a sense of wonder and curiosity about another. The experience is almost as though I, as the listener, can call forth the full expression of the 'listenee' simply by the way I listen to them. Sometimes I don't have to speak or ask questions but simply listen to their heart with my heart.

Listening to my own heart before speaking is another aspect of heart listening. It does not happen very often in ordinary conversation because it opens us up in ways that may be uncomfortable. Risking vulnerability with another takes courage. What if they take what I say and use it against me? What if they laugh at me? What if they ignore me?

The rewards of taking that risk are extraordinary. First, I experience the wonderful feeling of fully expressing my true self. Then I feel the intimacy and sense of relatedness with another. Connecting with someone on a heart level is a holy experience. Heart listening opens up what is sacred inside us, releasing love. Speaking and listening from the heart is the art of dialogue. The more I experience this kind of speaking and listening the more natural it becomes.

When I practise this sacred art I discover that the skills I learn can translate into my personal and professional lives. I find myself appreciating other points of view rather than being suspicious of them. I find others opening up to me in different ways. I feel more connected.

*Heart listening opens up what is sacred
inside us, releasing love.*

12

CREATING SAFE SPACES
Listening with love

What defines a safe space? Why do we need one? And how do we create one?

Safe spaces are especially important to facilitate listening when sensitive or controversial issues are being discussed. People need to feel that it's safe to express their opinions, that they can trust each other. It's harder to listen in tough situations if we don't first know the parameters of the conversation.

When I think I might be confronted about something or if I have to make a controversial decision, I will usually be busy planning my response instead of listening to the issue as it is presented. This changes if I know that there are guidelines for the conversation – that it's not going to be a free-for-all.

Commitment, respect and love make me feel safe to talk.

One of the first steps in creating safe space is finding a common commitment. A commitment can take many forms, but I find that a verbal understanding at the beginning of the conversation is the minimum for people to feel at ease. For instance, if I am meeting with a friend to dialogue about a recent incident that has troubled our relationship, our first task is to discover what we hope to accomplish. In this instance, it could be to heal our relationship, not necessarily to rehash the incident.

Another quality of safe space is respect for each other and for differing ways of expression. Even when we don't agree, we can honour the dignity of the human soul. It's not always easy to hear that which is counter to our opinions. And yet it is important for all to feel safe enough to share their ideas.

Perhaps the key quality of a safe space is love. One way to be sure that love is nurtured is to check in before you begin. Offer the opportunity for each person to say whatever he or she needs to in order to be present. Risk being vulnerable to deepen the possibility for connection. The trust that is generated from this process becomes a foundation for the rest of the conversation.

13

Listening with humility

The words 'humility' and 'humble' have been turning up frequently in my recent conversations. When we use the word 'humility' do we mean the act of being humble? What does it mean to be humble?

Often the word 'humble' is used to describe someone who lives a very simple life, someone untouched by materialism or consumerism, for example a monk or a nun. Or we may think of someone who is poor, who lives in humble surroundings.

Sometimes the word is used to admonish someone who is being arrogant: 'You should be more humble!' Or even to describe a defeat: 'They were humbled, brought to their knees.' Another word that comes to mind in these instances is 'humiliate'.

One of the roots of the word 'humility' is *humilis,* low or slight. Another is *humis,* earth or ground. This second root caught my attention.

What if a person who is humble is someone who is grounded, centred, someone who knows the power of Source and the interconnectedness of all beings? Could a humble person be one who considers all people as equals? Who isn't so concerned about what others say about him or her or about trying to impress others? An authentically humble person might be someone who is working on being true to Self. Maybe humility is about full self-expression, serving others by using one's own special gifts. Then, when you do something wonderful, you would naturally be thankful rather than boastful.

Listening with humility removes the urgent tug that we sometimes feel for conclusion and resolution in our conversations. When we learn to listen from the point of interconnectedness and service we truly hear what is said, rather than listening only long enough to give our response. Imagine a world with that kind of mutual support. This quality is embedded in deep listening.

I am reminded of the wisdom of Don Miguel Ruiz, a Toltec shaman, from his book *The Four Agreements:*

1. Be impeccable with your word.

2. Don't take anything personally.

3. Don't make assumptions.

4. Always do your best.

Express interconnectedness and service in mutual support.

14

PRACTISING PEACE
Listening to understand

'No peace among the nations without peace among the religions.' This statement by contemporary theologian Hans Küng has echoed in my mind ever since I first heard it. It is the spark that fuels the fire of my passion for dialogue with people of all the world's spiritual and religious traditions.

One important guideline of dialogue is listening to understand, not to agree with or believe. I do not have to agree with or believe what another person is saying in order to come to a new understanding of their experience.

Some time ago, I was at a small gathering of Christians from various denominations. There were also two Buddhists at the event. At one point during the weekend we paired off for a listening exercise, and one

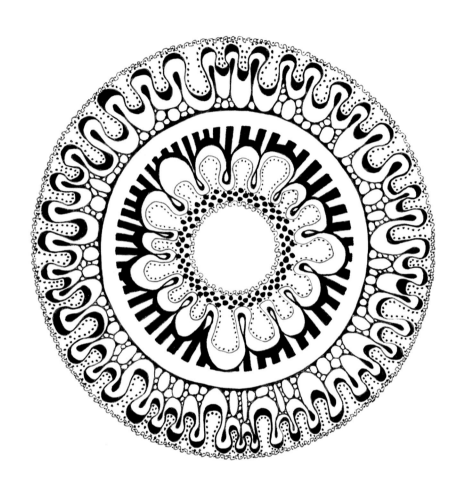

The more we trust, the more our hearts
open to love one another.

of the Buddhists and a Pentecostal Christian were partnered. Afterwards, the Pentecostal man told me about his experience in the dialogue. He reported that, at first, he was uneasy about talking through the issues at hand with the Buddhist. 'How will I be able to relate to someone who is not Christian, but who is committed to her own faith tradition?' he had wondered to himself. 'For a brief moment, I was tempted to begin a conversion conversation,' he said. 'But I realised that it was not appropriate.'

By the end of the exercise this sensitive Christian man discovered that he and his Buddhist partner were about as far apart as they could be in their beliefs, yet they were totally aligned in their values. The two of them left the gathering feeling completely related to each other.

Practitioners of dialogue have discovered three vital practices of listening to understand:

- The more we understand about one another, the less we fear.
- The less we fear, the more we trust.
- The more we trust, the more our hearts open to love one another.

15

CREATING HARMONY
Listening for integration

Many of us feel the need for more balance in our lives – balance between work and home, between partner and children, between body and spirit, and on and on. 'How to find balance in your life' is a common promise of articles, books and seminars on managing time in this fast-paced culture. The word 'balance' implies that there might be some magic formula which, if achieved in the right percentages, would lead to a fuller life of perfect equilibrium.

I used to view my life through the lens of balance. What were the different areas I wanted to keep in balance? How much was enough? How much was too much? Sometimes it seemed like a juggling act, and I wasn't a skilled juggler. The never-ending 'to do' list always interfered with the need for time to be still and reflect – to listen to the longing of the heart for harmony. Without inner harmony, we cannot listen to others with undivided attention and presence.

One day one of my daughters and I were talking about balance in life. We decided to replace the goal of balance with the practice of integration. What if we listened for the quality of integration in our lives? we asked ourselves. Our various activities would no longer have to fit on a balance scale; they would integrate with the whole.

Now I still have all of the same areas of life to manage: spiritual, family, physical, emotional, professional, community. But I no longer focus my energy on trying to discern the ideal percentage of time or energy to devote to one area over the other. A balanced whole is not simply the sum of its parts.

When I am listening with the essence of my soul, there is no separation into parts. Life is no longer a zero-sum game where putting more effort into one area means another area has to lose. Everything I do is related to the whole, and the transitions are more seamless. Each part nurtures the other instead of competing for my time and attention. Integration as distinct from balance leads us to harmony and peace, and from this peace we can listen – to Source, ourselves and others.

Everything I do is related to the whole.

16

Listening for insight

'The word is born in silence, and silence is the deepest response to the word.' These words from Catholic priest Henri Nouwen suggest that talking begins in silence, allowing us time to reflect. It is all too easy to say the first thing that comes to mind, rather than to look more deeply to see what is in the heart. Consciously being quiet and asking what wants to be said next is a discipline that yields wonderful fruit.

The same is true of listening. Reflection is important for both the speaker and the listener. As a speaker, I take a moment to look inside to see what really wants to be said, from my centre. As a listener, I am present with the speaker and, in the silence, ask what wants to be heard.

I am reminded of the Quaker saying, 'It is a sin to speak, if you're not moved to speak. It is also a sin not to speak, if you're moved to speak.'

I consciously choose to be quiet and ask myself
what wants to be said next.

I like to ask clarifying questions. But be mindful – what sometimes appears to be a clarifying question is actually a subtle tactic for moving one's own agenda. For example, the question 'Don't you think that…?' is rarely genuine. It is not a question that moves toward clarifying the ideas of the other person. The purpose of a clarifying question should be to lead to new levels of mutual understanding, to gain insight and perspective, not to confirm an already established opinion.

We need to be watchful with our assumptions. When someone speaks and we are not sure how to respond or react, we need to look at our assumptions and at how we are listening. Sometimes we notice that we are no longer listening to understand the other but are listening for agreement or debate. Sometimes we are assuming things about the other that are not so. When we remember that another's beliefs are as valid for him or her as ours are for us, insight opens.

17

SIMPLE SHARING

Listening for experiences

In the past few years, all forms of media have dramatically increased their coverage of spirituality. Spiritual experiences are discussed in everything from movies to major weekly newsmagazines to the local newspaper to books on the bestseller list. The National Institute for Healthcare Research announced that it would fund courses on spirituality at seven medical schools. On any given weekend, dozens of conferences, workshops and seminars are held on spirituality. What has happened?

One explanation comes from a most unlikely source – the World Economic Forum. A couple of years ago, the organisation sent teams to major think tanks around the world. The researchers concluded that at the root of capitalism is a spiritual bankruptcy, a conclusion that has been recognised by individuals around the world. The think tanks forecasted that there will be an intense search for spiritual values throughout the world between now and 2025.

A more recent survey, using the PsychoMatrix Spirituality Inventory, points to a deep interest and need for people to talk about the crucial issues concerning the meaning of life and the nature of death. These conversations call for small group settings or circles in which people share their stories. Listening deeply to Source, self and others is at the heart of this need. An undercurrent of sacred experience appears to be ready to surface.

Perhaps we are beginning to realise we are not alone, that we all share in the vagaries of life, that affirming values is important, and that a yearning for peace is universal. Creating safe spaces to share these experiences, developing ways to elicit stories of sacred experience, and encouraging compassionate action are the challenges and opportunities for all of us around the world.

Our lives are really about sacred experience.

18

Listening as caring

Caring is an aspect of love that can be seen in several forms across a broad spectrum from the personal, caring for myself, to the universal, caring for all creation. But our everyday language often works against our best motives as we strive to care. We so often use the word 'caring' as an act of disengagement: 'I couldn't care less,' 'I don't care,' or in the current slang, 'Whatever.'

We practise the sacred art of listening by looking for occasions to care. This can be challenging, even inconvenient. A dear friend of mine manages a business, and I had an opportunity to use her services. The work was completed, but the service I received did not fulfil my expectations. Since I value her friendship, I thought long and hard about what to do. Eventually, I wrote a long letter describing my experience honestly and

Caring for another often expresses our
listening in tangible ways.

with a deep sense of how much I care for her. I cared enough about her and our relationship to say things even though they were difficult to say. It worked. She did not respond with defensiveness, as we all so often do; she could see that I was caring for her.

Another incident occurred when one of my daughters ran the Los Angeles Marathon. The day of the race was cold, windy, rainy – one of the worst storms of the year – a perfect day to stay at home in front of the fireplace, curled up with a good book. I knew that if I phoned my daughter, she would say that it was okay if I excused myself because of the weather – but I also knew how important this race was to her. Listening to my inner voice told me that there was no question of my not going. Caring for my daughter got me out of the house for the miserable hour-and-a-half drive in a blinding rainstorm to be there.

Being there for my daughter and being honest with my friend are two examples of how listening to my inner voice manifested in caring. My listening resulted in specific actions. Caring for each other can be a physical, tangible reminder to those whom we listen to, confirming that we hear them. It is a demonstration of love in action.

19

HEARING NUANCES
Listening for each voice

'Diversity' is a word we use easily, whether it is diversity of race, culture, ethnicity, religion, sex, age, and so on. Awareness of diversity is growing, and we are urged to celebrate it. But for the past few years, I've grown uncomfortable with the popular notion of simply celebrating diversity. That seems ultimately limiting and superficial and doesn't allow for the calling forth of new possibilities for action or for a deepening sense of community.

What speaks to me instead is to find ways to honour and respect our differences through hearing the nuances in each particular voice. How can I learn more about the other? How can I learn to appreciate those who are different from me?

I was in a meeting recently where I quickly became aware of the broad diversity in styles of expression in the room. Not only were there differences of opinion, there were differences in the ways opinions were arrived at and expressed. I caught myself wondering, 'Why can't they all think like me?' Life would be much easier if we all thought alike. Or would it?

Then I realised that not only would such a world be boring, but it would dramatically limit our creative possibilities. I began to appreciate and listen for the different qualities of each speaker. I began to hear each voice as a part of the whole. That is diversity. Part of the tension of our differences is also the same thread that weaves us all together. If one voice is missing, we don't have a complete picture. The practice is to hear the voices for what they are – distinctive, individual. Imagine a three-dimensional sphere with threads criss-crossing, meeting and parting. If all parts are not in equal tension, the sphere cannot retain the shape of the whole.

So now I listen for nuances. When we hear each person's unique voice, we can better see their place as diverse individuals contributing to the whole. This is what we can create together when we listen deeply.

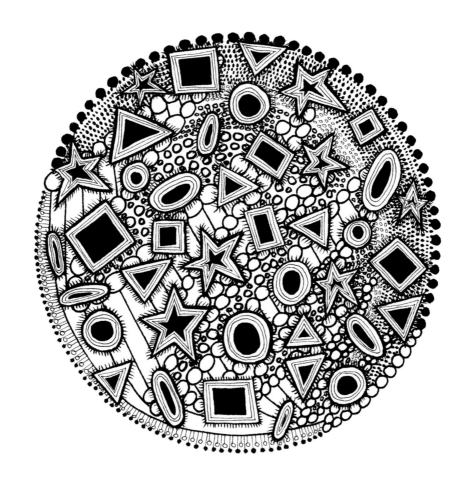

I began to hear each voice as a part of the whole.

20

Slowing Down
Listening to reflect

Think about a time when someone was truly listening to you, not just figuring out what to say next, wishing you would hurry up, or mentally reviewing a to-do list. He or she was just there, listening to you. Time stood still. A sense of the sacred was present. You felt understood, refreshed, whole, connected. What a rare experience in this fast-paced, information-based culture of the twenty-first century!

We are so busy running around doing things. The practice of stopping for a moment, being quiet, taking time to listen to the silence is not routine for most of us. And yet it is the silence out of which we listen more deeply. Listening for true wisdom to reveal itself is a slowing down, waiting, practising patience.

In my listening workshops I often present an exercise in which each person has the opportunity to respond to a different question. The

Slowing down prepares you to speak from the soul.

instructions are to repeat the question and then reflect for at least twenty to thirty seconds before speaking. On one occasion, a participant reported that he had an answer immediately, so he was sure he'd spend the rest of the time counting up to thirty. During the silence, however, he noticed that he continued to ask himself the question and looked deeper inside for a response. In the end, he was surprised at what he found himself saying. His was a profound experience, which he described as 'speaking from his soul.' Nearly every person who has attended these workshops has described a similar experience, as they learn to reflect before speaking.

It is important to slow down our thinking process, take time to reflect, listen to the still, small voice at the essence of our being, and open up the possibility of understanding. It not only takes time to listen like this, it takes practice to remember to do so. The blessing comes in feeling profoundly related to others, especially those whose beliefs are different from our own.

21

THE VOICE WITHIN
Listening for change

Can listening – and other sacred arts of conversation and relationship – help to create a less violent world? Absolutely.

The United Nations has declared the first decade of the new century the Decade for a Culture of Peace and Nonviolence for the Children of the World. The representatives of more than twenty nations are calling for a future without war. We all hope for a world at peace, a world in which every voice counts, a world in which we recognise our inter-dependence, a world in which the value of our relationships is the key to resolving our differences. Yet how do these vague hopes translate into changes in our daily life?

Notice how we use language to describe events, other people and ourselves. Amazingly, words like 'hate', 'kill' or 'shoot' are part of daily conversation. 'Don't you just hate it when…' 'That just about killed me.' 'Well, shoot!' We create campaigns and battle plans for the fight to win market share or increased revenue. We talk about wars on poverty, crime and drugs.

Another place we see violence is in our thoughts. As I drive up and down our freeways, rushing to get somewhere, how do I respond to the person who sneaks in front of me at the last minute while I'm patiently waiting in the exit lane? Or the solo driver in the car-pool lane? Or the one speeding by on the shoulder while the rest of us are at a standstill?

Am I willing to take the time to slow down, breathe, and ask myself if what I'm about to do or say will violate someone or something? Am I willing to listen to what I don't want to hear and still respond with respect, compassion and love instead of fighting back? Am I willing to admit that nurturing nonviolence in the world begins with listening to those places in me where I can nurture peace?

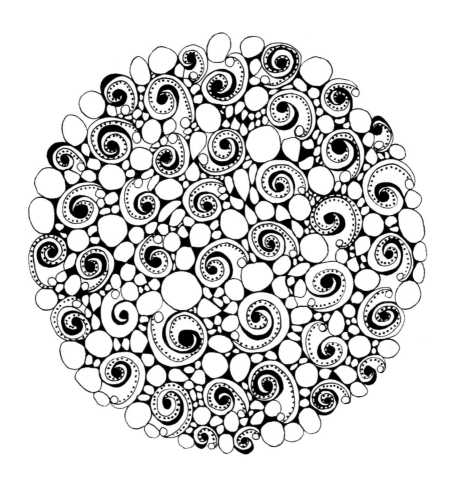

Nurturing nonviolence in the world begins with listening
to those places in me where I can nurture peace.

22

ASSUMPTIONS
Listening for clarity

Effective listening is enhanced when we learn to suspend assumptions. At first glance this sounds fairly easy to do. But recognising our own assumptions can be slippery. How do we know when we are assuming something about the speaker or about what's being said? What is an 'assumption', anyway?

There is a certain transparency to assumptions. We are making assumptions when we take for granted that we already know what the speaker is talking about or what the other person is going to say. The result is that we stop listening to understand and begin listening to our own internal conversation about what we imagine is being said. Another clue that an assumption is getting in the way of our listening is when we have an emotional response to what is being said.

I discover that what I assumed is quite different
from what the speaker intended.

When we notice that assumptions are taking over, what would be an authentic or heart response? One way is simply to acknowledge the assumptions silently, suspend them for the time being, and return to listening. But sometimes that isn't enough. We may need to identify the assumption and, when the speaker is finished, articulate the assumption or ask a clarifying question to see if the assumption is accurate. It is often a compliment to the speaker to find out that they are being listened to with such attention.

Many times I discover that my assumptions are quite different from the speaker's intentions. Taking time to clarify the issue clears the space for greater understanding. This does not always mean that I have come to agree with the other's position, but I find that I can appreciate the other's perspective in the light of clarity.

Listening for clarity can be taken to a very basic level in everyday conversations. Have you ever noticed how often you have been interrupted in mid-sentence by someone who assumes they know what you are going to say? Or vice versa? Slow down, take time to listen, and listen for clarity, quieting your assumptions.

23

LEARNING FROM PASSION
Listening for vision

In my conversations I like to ask people meaningful questions, for instance, 'Why are we here?' Questions like this one invite us to think about what we want, not about what we don't want. I also like to ask, 'What would it be like if…?' and 'What is your vision for the future?' We can experience hope, life and energy in this kind of enquiry as we discover our passion and vision.

As we listen to each other in our relationships we expand our vision when we help each other focus our attention on what we are looking for. We are trained to focus our attention on what's wrong or what's not working so that we can begin fixing it. We're problem solvers. Sometimes we fall into thinking that listening without problem solving is wasting time. But too often we find problems wherever we look, asking, 'Why did this happen? Who's to blame?' Sacred listening is interested in much more than that. Our job is to listen for each other's vision, to focus on our fundamental values and strengths.

One day a friend and I were talking about a community project she was working on. Nothing was going right. All she could see were problems. As I listened I began to hear that underneath her complaints was a deep passion for making a difference in her community. So rather than focus on solving her problems, I said, 'How did you get involved in this project? What was it that appealed to you? Tell me about your hopes and dreams for this community.' As she responded to these questions she began to find new possibilities for taking action, and her original enthusiasm and excitement were reignited.

As we practise listening we can pose questions to create openings. For example, we can ask, 'What is it that, if it were present, would lead to what we want?' This calls for creativity, energy, and looking for what is possible, not just what is wrong. These questions guide us to focus on our greatness instead of on our weakness.

This may sound too simple, but it's at the core of our spiritual lives. Our passion will tell us how to take action and will guide us to a vision for our entire life.

Listening often means looking for what is possible.

24

Contemplative Prayer
Listening for guidance

Contemplative prayer is the practice of listening to God. When we practise this kind of listening, we are also preparing ourselves to listen to our own inner voice and to each other.

Contemplation begins when our whole being is open to a Presence beyond words, thought and emotions. For many of us, prayer is associated with talking to God – we speak and God listens. Mother Teresa had a different approach. She said, 'We need to find God, and he cannot be found in noise and restlessness. God is the friend of silence.'

In order to facilitate contemplation, some people find that leading into the silence with music, chanting or reading is a useful transition. There are many contemplative practices that provide access to this kind of prayer and sacred intention. Several examples are centring prayer,

Daily practice in listening to the sacred voice prepares me
to listen to my own inner voice and to others.

walking meditation, walking the labyrinth, saying the rosary or other counted prayers, singing a kirtan, meditating by focusing on your breathing or on a still point like a candle flame, chanting, reciting the repetitive phrase of the Jesus prayer, the sacred sound of Om, or meditating on the names of God.

I recommend a daily contemplative practice of some kind to everyone I counsel. I would go so far as to say that it is an essential practice for the sacred art of listening.

The fruits of contemplative practice are many:

- We learn to discern what really matters and to let go of what does not.
- We are less likely to judge other people.
- We accept our own basic goodness.
- We cultivate an open mind.
- We transform our motivations and purify our intentions.
- We achieve inner freedom to serve truthfully in the outer world.

Find a practice that works for you and make a commitment to it. Practise for at least thirty consecutive days. Your life will be transformed by an increased awareness of God's presence and a deepening sense of gratitude and appreciation. Your ability to listen deeply to yourself and to others will never be the same.

25

The Agenda-free Conversation
Listening with openness

Listening doesn't always happen when two or more people are talking. Conversations can be like tag-team monologues, each person waiting for the other to stop speaking so that each can take turns presenting their case. There's not much listening for understanding going on when each side is trying to convince the other that their position is the right one, or that they have the answer, or that they know what's best for you. Why listen? Why talk?

Letting go of the desire to be right or to be nice or to seek approval, not only when listening but also when speaking, takes work. Guidelines for successful talking and listening are designed to remind us of the purpose of dialogue – to listen for understanding, to share and exchange ideas, and to seek new insights that were not present at the start. It takes practice to loosen our attachments to our own agendas.

In my experience, using 'I' language is the path to learning this lesson of listening with openness. At first this was an uncomfortable practice for me. All of my training had taught me that speaking or writing 'I' was not correct, that it was egocentric. Then I began to realise that the 'I' in this instance was not the ego clamouring for attention but the heart yearning to be heard.

One of the hardest places for me to practise letting go of my agenda is when my husband and I talk politics. We are often on opposite sides of an issue. I find myself wanting to convince him that I'm right or wondering why he can't see the correctness of my position. The conversation can quickly deteriorate unless I remember to practise what I teach. As I listen to what he is saying, letting go of my need to be right, I can begin to understand why he supports or opposes an issue, that his commitment is as valid for him as mine is for me, and, sometimes, that we actually agree on certain aspects. Then when I speak, I am able to speak from my heart without any expectation of convincing him, simply sharing what is so for me.

When I honour that voice in myself and in others I begin to lose my attachment to a predetermined outcome. By taking responsibility for what I say and letting go of my agenda to convince the other person, I am able to hear them more honestly. Our hearts open and connect.

*When I honour that voice in myself and in others, I begin
to lose my attachment to a predetermined outcome.*

26

Listening without prejudice

Southern California, where I live, is home to people from all over the world. Sometimes it seems as if we have more diversity than almost anywhere else on the planet. The United States itself is becoming one of the most religiously and culturally diverse countries in history. We come from a staggering number of varying backgrounds. How do we learn to listen to each other when cultural and religious practices and beliefs are so different?

I reflected on this question during a recent vacation in another country. We travelled by many modes of transportation and were often in a crowd of people. In America, we have been trained to line up and board on a first-come, first-served basis. It seems a fair and equitable way to manage large groups of people. Think about the queues at Disneyland!

Listening with love is possible when I see
differences for what they are.

The first time we waited to board a bus, I was surprised to find no line, just a sort of gigantic huddle. When the bus arrived, there was mild chaos as everyone good-naturedly pushed and shoved to get on board. Somehow we all managed to get on. At first, I was shocked at what I considered rude behaviour. In another instance, when we were standing in a line waiting to be helped, several people marched right up to the front and – brazenly, from my point of view – crashed the line. How arrogant, I thought.

It was up to me to learn that these were cultural patterns, not personal vendettas against me. Certainly these differences were not indicators of morality or goodness. I had to look beyond my familiar assumptions if I was going to have any hope of listening for the heart of people who are different from me. Only then could I begin to have a relationship with them.

This scenario even plays out at the smallest levels on a daily basis. My husband folds the towels one way. I fold them another. Is he being uncooperative and arrogant? No, we simply have different approaches. Sometimes we may have to remind ourselves of this over and over. Listening with love is not possible if we cannot see differences for what they are.

27

ATTENTION
Listening for perspective

Listening is a lost art. When people ask me what I do, they often respond by saying, 'Yes, we could all use some help in listening.' Or, 'Will you talk to my husband/wife/boss/kids?' Sometimes it seems as if no one is listening. The author Ernest Hemingway advised, 'When people talk, listen completely. Most people never listen.'

According to the International Listening Association, research studies indicate that we spend about 45 percent of our time listening, but we are distracted, preoccupied or forgetful about 75 percent of that time. The average attention span for adults is twenty-two seconds. Immediately after listening to someone talk, we usually recall only about half of what we heard. Within a few hours we remember about 20 percent of what we've heard. Less than 5 percent of us have had any training in listening skills. As a manager of a large business said once, 'I have always prepared myself to speak. But I have never prepared myself to listen.'

We have forgotten how to listen. We have the distractions of television, computers, mobile phones and pagers, and we have countless activities to fit into our days. With all of this going on, it sometimes feels as if the world is spinning out of control. Who has the time to slow down and smell the roses? And yet we seem to know on a deeper level that we need to take time out and regroup – maybe go on a retreat. The practice of being quiet would give us some breathing time. Good idea, but then a retreat becomes one more thing to schedule in.

Another alternative is a mini-retreat, a brief time out in the midst of daily life. Mini-retreats are a conscious way for me to explore my inner life, to take the time to listen to God or Spirit, to slow down enough so I can hear and acknowledge or question what God is doing in my life. It's a way to regain perspective and to balance the calmness and peace of my inner life with the fast pace and sometimes chaotic nature of my outer life.

Try one of these mini-retreat practices:

- Go outside and listen for the birds for one minute.
- Sit down in a chair while you wait for water to boil for tea or coffee. Notice all the sounds you hear.
- Next time you're stuck in traffic, practise patience and compassion.
- Take two minutes of silence before or after lunch.
- Put on your favorite CD and sit down to listen to it.

Give yourself permission to do nothing else while you are on mini-retreat. Take a break from multi-tasking.

For me, these shifts in perspective often occur through nature – when I look up and see a rainbow or a spectacular sunset. I shift from rushing around chasing deadlines to being in a calm place of deep gratitude and blessing.

These quiet times nurture our souls and prepare us to listen with our ears, eyes and hearts – and with undivided attention. The Sufi poet Hafiz offers this wisdom: 'How do I listen to others? As if everyone were my Master speaking to me.'

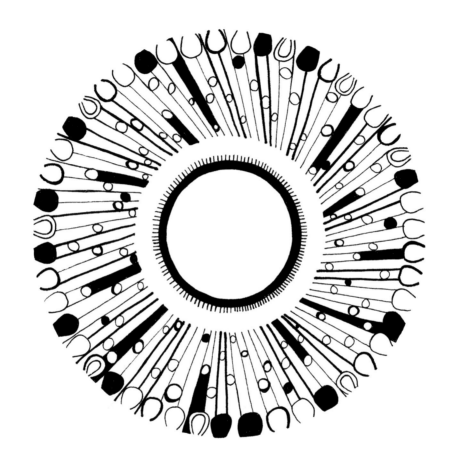

Quiet times nurture our souls and prepare us to listen.

28

Hospitality
Listening as a gift

The word 'hospitality' conveys the image of receiving a guest with open arms or simply being kind to guests and strangers. Not long ago, I returned from a weekend out of town where I was the recipient of magnificent hospitality. I felt so cared for and nurtured.

As I reflected on my experience I realised that hospitality goes beyond being kind and making someone feel welcome. My hosts had attended to the smallest detail of my stay prior to my arrival, so the hospitality began before I even left home. What a gift!

While I was there I had the freedom just to be present, the same freedom I want my friends to feel when they are talking to me about their greatest concerns, joys, fears. It was a reminder of the importance of attention — of being attentive to another's welfare — in every interaction and conversation.

As listeners, we offer a space for others
to feel free to be themselves.

I had another insight about receiving hospitality during the workshop I presented on that trip. At the closing, a participant offered a suggestion about the way I began one of the exercises. My first thought was to explain why I did what I did. Then I stopped, listened, and realised that he was really offering me a gift – a contribution – and my job was to receive it gracefully.

Listening is one of the greatest gifts we give to each other. Practise this gift of hospitality in your daily life:

- When you're in the post office, take a minute to really listen to the person who's talking with you.
- At your job, really listen when your co-worker makes a comment.
- At home, stop whatever you're doing when your family members talk to you.

When we listen deeply to another person we are practising hospitality. We are offering a space for others to feel free to be themselves and to change and grow in their understanding.

Imagine a world where we all treated each other like guests, extending grace and generosity of spirit. By practising hospitality we can create an environment for conversation where people feel safe enough to talk and are grateful to listen.

29

FOCUS
Listening for the holy

Lately, my life has been in the midst of one of those 'too much' times – much too much to do in much too little time. Have you ever noticed that when there are too many projects or tasks, too many appointments to keep or calls to make, it's hard to get started on anything? When this happens to me, I often find myself immobilised and nothing happens except in my mind, where I worry, fret, make mental lists, wonder how I'm going to get it all done.

One way that I remedy this state is to reset my focus. I choose one task and do it. When this works I enter into a state of seeing only what is in front of me. My relationship with time and space shifts, and I work on the one task that's right there. The chatter disappears. I complete that task and move on to the next one. Focus.

What is focus, exactly? How can we get into that space more often? Interestingly enough, the word 'focus' comes from the Latin word for fireplace or hearth. When I think of 'focus' from this perspective, I begin to see a spiritual approach for managing the 'too much' state. The hearth at the centre of a room is like the heart at the centre of my being.

In listening, focus is similar to mindfulness. By quieting the chatter in our heads and focusing on the centre of our being, not only can we move forward with each task but also we can see through the clutter in our relationships to hear the holiness that is there. For me, focus is like tuning in to Source. When I am connected, everything becomes sacred – holy. There is a flow and ease to what I'm doing, even though I may be working very hard.

Focus changes the context in which we are working from one of chaos to one of serenity. The external work may not look so different, yet it's being done from a different place. We are at peace. We listen for the holy and enter the sacred space of flow and harmony.

I listen for the holy and enter the sacred space
of flow and harmony.

30

ENGAGE FIRST
Listening beyond appearances

We are all familiar with the saying 'Don't judge a book by its cover.' I was reminded of it yet again in a recent encounter.

I accompanied a friend to the dentist's office to give her some moral support. We were in the waiting room when a young woman walked in and sat down nearby. She immediately made a call on her cell phone. Her voice became louder and louder as if amplified by a microphone.

My friend and I exchanged glances. I was wondering how I could say something to this woman to let her know how intrusive she was being. I pegged her as a thoughtless, inconsiderate Generation Xer. Fortunately, the call was not long. When it ended my friend and I were relieved and yet still somewhat annoyed. We chose to engage her in a conversation, rather than complain, hoping to discover more about her – and to help

Superficial judgements about people keep us
from seeing them for who they are.

us understand her behaviour. As she told her story we got to know a wonderful young woman who had been through a lot in her life. She was thoughtful, considerate, and really quite delightful. The cause of our discomfort became less important than connecting with another human being. Engaging first is about listening to each other's stories.

My original judgement had been inaccurate and misguided. How often do we make assumptions like these without ever having the opportunity to find out that we're wrong? How many people do we write off or deliberately ignore, only because they look a certain way or behave a certain way?

To suspend prejudgement, to be present, to take time to be in the moment, to look for opportunities to connect – without being foolhardy or naive – is a challenge. But we cannot begin to truly listen if we do not first engage with one another. A simple lesson, but only when we drop our superficial judgements about people will we begin to see them for who they are – and be able to hear what they have to say.

31

THE CHALLENGE OF CHANGE
Listening creatively

Have you ever noticed that just when life is going well and you think that you have things under control, something happens and you have to start all over again? Or reprioritise? Or reschedule? Or be more flexible than is comfortable?

Change – it's inevitable, and yet somehow it often comes as a surprise. Even knowing that change is one of the certainties of life doesn't make it any easier to accept.

I have noticed that some changes are easy for me, while others throw me off guard. Sometimes, our ability to adapt depends on how the rest of the day is going. On good days we can tolerate a lot of change. On hectic days one more change can send us reeling.

And yet the sacred art of listening is all about change. Creating something that didn't exist before cannot happen without change. Any new relationship or opportunity for listening generates change.

At one point in my life I was assigned to a group responsible for creating a new, nonhierarchical management structure within an organisation. We came up with a wonderful design and began to put it into practice. However, at the first roadblock, my brain reverted to its default position of previous models of thinking. I really had to work to pull myself away from that pattern to look at what might be possible if we did things in this new way. It's remarkable how the uncertainty of something new makes us cling to the familiar, a life raft in a sea of change. I was able to talk and listen freely only when I completely accepted an environment of change.

When we find ourselves thinking we have to do things a certain way, or we hear ourselves saying, 'That's not the way we do it here' or 'It's not going to work,' stop and ask a question. Is it really true, or are we simply uncomfortable with a change? Listening creatively happens when we open our hearts to others in wonder, appreciation and awe.

Entering any new relationship opens us to change, too. A whole new world of freedom, possibility and creativity emerges when we can listen to change.

A whole new world of freedom, possibility and creativity emerges when we can listen to change.

32

RELATIONSHIPS
Listening for deeper connections

One of the joys and blessings of life is making authentic connections with people, creating relationships. I am doubly blessed as I experience this in my work with people from different cultures, countries and backgrounds.

Recently I attended a global gathering of representatives from the various world religions. Participants came from all over the world, and despite our apparent differences friendships developed quickly. We worked in small groups throughout the week, discussing a variety of topics. Those at my table were from New Delhi, Manapur in northeast India, Belgium, Nairobi, San Francisco, Taos and southern California. We quickly became a global family of brothers and sisters.

Five of the women with whom I became close were from Germany, Pakistan, Uganda, Argentina and Iran. These women are now part of my

Creating relationships is making authentic connections with people.

global family. They are my sisters. Each time I read a newspaper or hear a news report on the radio or television, I realise that it is my family who is being talked about. These relationships developed out of spending time with each other, hearing each other's stories, eating meals together.

I wish that my relationships at home were always so seemingly effortless. But I think oftentimes it is harder to forge deep connections when we live close together. We focus too much on what must get done, where we must be going.

The importance of relationship is central to all of our work – whoever we are, wherever we are and whatever we do. Yet relationship is often relegated to last place rather than first. How many times have you been in a meeting where getting through the agenda is the highest priority? Where taking time to check in with everyone or even to introduce the people who are present is seen as a waste of time? I question the long-term effectiveness of work that is done in a vacuum of relationship. In contrast, imagine what it would be like if we truly became connected with the people in our meetings, our offices, our lives. If we took the time to say, 'Hello, how are you?' and waited for the response, if we requested that people introduce themselves at the beginning of each meeting, if we stopped and welcomed and introduced the late arrivals as a way to include everyone, if our relationships received top priority, if we were able to discover that what impacts one impacts all, I expect that deep listening would come more naturally to us.

33

THE GIFT OF SOLITUDE
Listening to the silence

What is solitude? Is it vanishing from daily life? Sometimes. Can solitude happen in the midst of daily life with all its distractions? Sometimes. Can solitude be shared with others? Sometimes. The longer I live, the more I yearn for this thing called solitude. I also see it as an important practice in learning to listen well.

Solitude is about being with myself – alone. Solitude gives me a sense of quietness and peace, a feeling of stillness and joy in my heart. It is from this place of listening in silence that I start to recognise the voice of God. The more I listen, the more I trust that voice. I begin to know myself in the process. I am inspired to action.

I experience solitude when I am all alone in my house. No radio, tele-vision, music or computer – simply the silence of being. It is delicious.

The mystics of each spiritual tradition have written about this way of tapping into God's silence. I think that listening begins here, in the stillness of my heart.

Sometimes solitude comes to me when I'm driving. There is that moment of being fully present to life – seeing the wonder of humanity or nature or God's presence in the world and in my life. Many times, solitude is in the shared silence with a close friend, spouse or family member. Just being with each other, not needing to speak.

'Why do you suppose these moments of solitude offer us such relief? Because they give us a chance to simply be ourselves, to enjoy what and where we are, to savour just being. Alone with God, we feel no need to perform, to do,' writes Frank Bianco in his book *Voices of Silence*.

How can you find the time to take on another practice in your already fully scheduled day? One woman discovered that if she spent just one minute in silence before getting out of the car before and after work, it made a difference in her day. She was more centred in the office and in her home. This practice of solitude, of being still, silent, and present, expands awareness and leads to a deeper relationship with the Divine as well as a deeper capacity to be with others. Take advantage of the gift of quiet time. Enjoy.

A feeling of stillness creates space for joy in my heart.

34

Listening for the questions

One of the goals that is emphasised in our culture is finding answers – solving problems, answering questions, removing doubt. We want to know who, what, when, where and why – and we want to know now. When we listen, we are trained to listen for the answers.

A friend of mine who is a schoolteacher told me about a study that reported the average amount of time between a teacher asking a question and then calling on a student for the answer to be one second or less. One second or less! The researchers wanted to test another idea, so they asked teachers to wait at least seven seconds before calling on someone. What the teachers and administrators discovered was that the students who rarely raised their hands began to do so, and the quality and depth of each response increased noticeably. At an early age, we can learn to reflect before we answer.

Practise listening for your inner voice.

Reflective listening distinguishes a response from an answer. It is a practice to get to know your inner voice, and it takes time and patience.

First, take a few breaths before responding to a situation, question or comment. In those few seconds, ask yourself what wants to happen next. Then wait for your inner voice to respond. Remember that you are not listening for the answer; you are listening for a response, for your true wisdom to reveal itself.

Most important, as you practise reflection, notice that what you want to say (the ego) matters less than what wants to be said (the soul). Reflective listening is a slowing down, waiting, practising patience with yourself.

Reflective listening is also about listening for the questions. We are constantly pulled away from our innermost self and encouraged to look for answers instead of listening for the questions. Rainer Maria Rilke's advice to the young poet was, 'Live the question now. Perhaps you will then gradually, without noticing it, live along some day into the answer.'

The practice of listening for the questions – for what wants to be said next – deepens your relationship to your inner voice, your soul, and enhances full self-expression.

35

A SACRED MEETING PLACE
Listening through prayer

I was talking with a group of Cambodian refugees about the power of prayer and the possibility of being more intentional about praying for peace. I had been invited to their church to teach them Centring Prayer. As we spoke they decided to commit one day a month to fasting and praying for peace. This immediate response of taking action really touched me.

As I was driving home I reflected on how much praying matters. I thought about studies in the healthcare field that show that people who are being prayed for improve more rapidly than those who are not. Similarly, I pondered, can praying for peace in the world make a healing difference to the ways that we listen to each other?

The United Religions Initiative, an organisation dedicated to creating cultures of peace in the world through interfaith cooperation at a grassroots level, invokes this prayer:

> Supreme One, who has made of one blood all peoples to dwell upon the earth, our thanks and praise for deepening the understanding of those of all races, languages, customs and religions and for teaching us to accept each other in the light of your own all-embracing love. Thank you also for the vision of all the human family united in caring partnership and stewardship for the sake of all life and the earth.

'Never doubt for a minute that a small group of people can change the world. Indeed it has never happened any other way,' says the anthropologist Margaret Mead.

'Intention…triggers transformation of energy and information. Intention organises its own fulfilment,' writes Deepak Chopra.

Perhaps we learn to listen when we pray before the One who hears all. Our intentions can shape what happens. We listen to each other when we meet in prayer.

Our intentions can shape what happens.

36

RECOGNISING INTOLERANCE
Listening for your humanity

Two events in my life caused me to question the depth of my own tolerance for other people's beliefs. The first is very personal. One of my daughters recently became a 'born again' Christian and joined a fundamentalist group that does not acknowledge the validity of other faith traditions or spiritual paths, including my own. Aside from being unsettled by this decision, I was dismayed to discover the hidden intolerance lurking deep down inside of me toward members of these groups. I had thought I was fairly open and tolerant. But my soul-searching led me to a new understanding of what it means to be tolerant – and to truly live one of the cardinal rules of good listening: 'Listen for understanding, not to agree with or believe.' I now know and respect that my daughter's faith is a deeply meaningful experience for her, and we can authentically

*Open the door for relationships that
include our differences.*

communicate about her spiritual journey. I am also noticing that many times we are simply using different words to describe very similar experiences. When I translate what she says into my experience, my language, I can usually relate to it. And when I translate what I say into her experience, language that she understands, we find our common ground. It's like being an interpreter of a foreign language.

The other experience that led me to question my own tolerance happened at a local interfaith council meeting where spiritual issues that cut across religious lines are discussed. One of the council members proposed that we take a stand on a controversial issue and assumed that all of us would agree. She expressed surprise when the agreement was not unanimous. Another council member expressed the opinion that once people were enlightened or transformed they would certainly see the rightness of the proposed position. In the midst of our interfaith council for religious tolerance was explicit intolerance! Finally, another council member suggested that perhaps the purpose of our group was not to take positions but to be a safe forum where differing opinions could be expressed.

These two experiences led me to consider how I can manage to be tolerant of those who are intolerant of my beliefs. I don't have the answers. But I know that when we listen for the humanity that is beyond the intolerance, when we can appreciate the essence of light in each other, it opens the door for relationships that include our differences – even the subtle and the most difficult ones.

37

PATIENCE
Listening with intention

Patience is necessary for deep listening. Have you ever noticed how hard it is to slow down enough to really hear what someone is saying? Or to sustain your interest for more than a minute or so?

My mind always seems to be way ahead of the speaker. This is not surprising, since the average person speaks at the rate of 120 to 150 words per minute but our brains can process more than 500 words per minute. It takes patience to remain present with the speaker.

The importance of patience was very noticeable to me at a conference I attended that was conducted by First Nations (indigenous) people in Canada. Thirty-five of us spent two and a half days in a talking circle. The elders took turns sharing teachings, and then the talking stick would make its way around the circle. Many times it took more than two hours to complete the process.

All went well for about the first half of the circle, then my mind started to wander. I found myself hoping that the people in the second half of the circle would be very brief – or pass the stick because they had nothing to add to the conversation. I'd get irritated when someone would go on and on, giving illustration after illustration of the same point. Sometimes it seemed as if we'd never finish! It was hard to stay put in my chair.

The lesson for me—and for several others, as I discovered in the debriefing time—was to listen to each person with attentiveness, to listen with the intention of learning something new and to let go of my attachment to time. I also realised that often one of the last speakers had a point that was exactly what I needed to hear or that opened up a new insight for me.

I invite you to take this practice into daily life situations. Notice when you begin to get restless as someone else is speaking. Refocus your attention on her or him. Find something to appreciate in what is being said. Listen with an expectation that you will gain insight. Wake up! Practising patience leads to deeper connections and greater understanding.

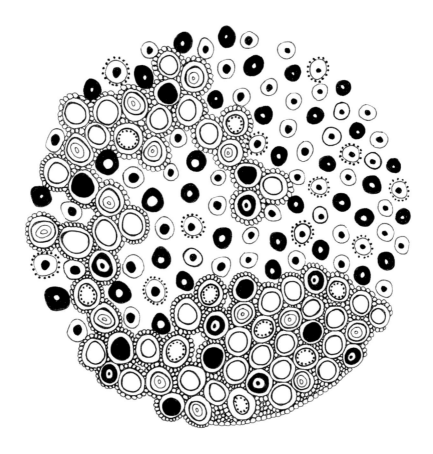

Practising patience leads to moments of revelation
that we might otherwise miss.

38

Harvest Time
Listening with gratitude

In the United States of the twenty-first century, many local communities of diverse religious groups come together to celebrate the Thanksgiving holiday. Some develop a special service, with each spiritual leader taking a part. All of these inspiring communities share their traditions in music and demonstrate hospitality with food and drink.

I love these moments. There is a quality about breaking bread together that also breaks down barriers between us. In a similar way, when I sit down next to someone unknown to me and just start talking, something wonderful happens. The one who had been a stranger – either because he or she looked different, dressed or talked differently, or worshipped in a different faith – soon becomes a friend. I discover we have universal

Demonstrate listening by showing gratitude.

concerns about life, about how we teach values to our children, about what we can do to promote harmony and peace where we live.

The Supreme Patriarch of Cambodian Buddhists, Maha Ghosananda, when asked for his thoughts about peace, said, 'We are one. We are all in the same boat.' The boat is planet Earth. How can we all live together as one while still maintaining our distinct traditions and beliefs?

We start by listening to each other with gratitude. It can be as simple as a smile, wave or nod of greeting. It can be writing a letter to the editor or acknowledging your favourite author or columnist. It can be inviting your neighbours over for coffee and dessert. The possibilities are endless! It is a valuable practice to find creative, simple ways to show that we listen and are grateful for what we have found.

39

BEING YOURSELF
Listening with authenticity

As we learn to listen more completely we may find ourselves noticing that there are a lot of people in our lives who could learn to listen better. The sacred art of listening is an individual journey, so each person enters and learns at his or her own pace and desire. Until a person is ready, what we can do is listen from our own hearts, with no expectation that he or she will then listen to us in return. This simple act of letting go often opens the door for a subtle shift in your relationship, which then translates into deeper communication.

Just as marriage experts explain that the worst thing we can do to our partner in conversation is to try to solve all of his or her problems, so too in every listening relationship it is wise to avoid presumptions. We demonstrate that we care when we are content just to listen. The quality of our listening has more impact on the relationship than anything we can do or say.

A mutually enriching conversation, a true dialogue, is more about 'being' – being oneself and being present with another, being open to some new understanding – than it is about 'doing it right'. When we cannot honestly be ourselves with another person, we cannot really listen.

In my consultations with people through The Listening Center, I have heard first-hand the many rewards of learning to feel comfortable being ourselves in conversation. Each person reports that they listen to people more openly when they practise this way.

One woman reported that when she's authentically being herself she finds that she better appreciates others for being who they are, rather than trying to make them into her idea of who they should be.

Another friend described an incident that happened when her employer was downsizing and a number of employees were being terminated. The company offered a severance package that did not seem fair to her. She said that her experience of practising this principle of good dialogue gave her the tools to speak out without attacking anyone. The company officers were so impressed with what she said that they met with her privately, and the final package was changed – for everyone!

When we remember to practise the simple art of being ourselves, we listen to others with the wisdom of our true hearts. In all of your relationships keep asking yourself, 'Am I listening with my authentic Self?'

Listening is called a spiritual practice because it requires daily attention. We practise to build other capacities, like love, hope and faith – and we don't ever reach a point where we can stop practising. There is no upper tier, no graduation from the sacred art of listening.

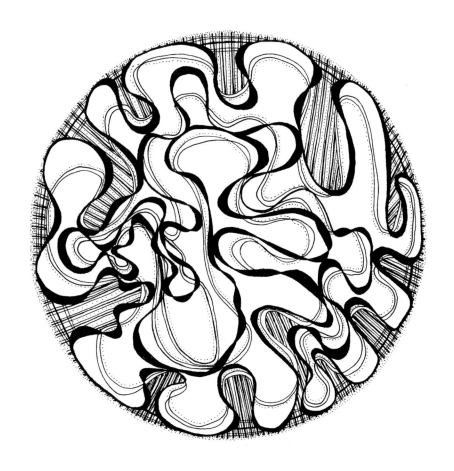

Our authentic Self listens with wisdom.

40

BEING COMPLETE
Listening beyond the past

A new month, a new year, a new birth, even a death – these are times to think about new beginnings. We are offered another chance to start again, unencumbered by the past. 'This time it's going to be different' is one of our frequent refrains.

These reminders work for me for a while but then, all too often, I notice that I am back into old patterns where the 'new' looks a lot like the familiar patterns of the past.

I have discovered that sometimes the reason why nothing seems to change in my life is that something is unresolved in my past. I find that I am carrying my past with me into the future. And so I've learned to spend time taking stock of the past, acknowledging what happened, and looking to see what I need to do to bring it to completion. Sometimes

Sometimes being complete is as simple as saying so.

being complete is as simple as saying so. Other times I write about issues in my journal or I contact by letter, phone or in person those with whom I am incomplete. This opens a fresh, clean place for creating.

Our capacity to move beyond the past was demonstrated beautifully to me when I was in Cape Town, South Africa, attending the Parliament of the World's Religions. A black taxi driver told me that ten years ago he would not have been allowed to drive. Now he can drive and even own his own car. He talked about his four children who are all in school. He told me he was so happy they are learning English, which was not allowed to be taught to blacks during apartheid. He acknowledged the problems and yet was hopeful for the future. The past was not dominating his thinking.

May we all start a new day complete with the past, so we will be free to create our future in peace and harmony with all that is.

Part Three

In Closing

LISTENING IN YOUR WORLD

The purpose of this book of illustrated reflections on learning the sacred art of listening is to illuminate your spiritual journey by providing an entry to a new but ancient way of being with Source, yourself and others.

The sacred art of listening is something to incorporate in your life and use every day. The following questions are designed to add to your understanding and to encourage you to take what you have learned into your life and into the world. Return to these questions again and again as you deepen your spiritual practice.

- Where does listening show up missing in my life?
- What is a conversation that I want or need to have?
- With whom?

You are also invited to participate in the ongoing evolution of the art of listening. We would like to hear your stories.

- How did you use this book?
- What was the most valuable insight you had while reading it?
- What new possibilities opened up for you?
- What additional topics for reflection occurred to you?

You are welcome to share your own experiences with *The Sacred Art of Listening* by contacting the author, Kay Lindahl, at The Listening Center.
E-mail: kay@sacredlistening.com
Fax: (949) 496-5535
Mail: P.O. Box 6805, Laguna Niguel, CA 92607-6805, USA
Website: www.sacredlistening.com

PRINCIPLES OF DIALOGUE
Nine guidelines for listening to others

The following guidelines have been developed as a result of more than ten years of practising dialogue in a grassroots interfaith community, the Alliance for Spiritual Community, and in my work leading The Listening Center, which offers classes, workshops and retreats on the sacred art of listening to people of all faiths and backgrounds.

My own teachers and mentors include Dr David Bohm, a physicist who became interested in the way humans learn and think, particularly collectively. Over the years he developed a deep understanding of true conversation, which he called dialogue.

These guidelines are designed to facilitate healthy dialogue and deep listening in various situations and to create a safe space for meaningful conversation on all levels.

1. **When you are listening, suspend assumptions.** What we assume is often invisible to us. We assume that others have had the same experiences that we have, and that's how we listen to them. Learn to recognise assumptions by noticing when you get upset or annoyed by something someone else is saying. You may be making an assumption. Let it be – suspend it – and resume listening for understanding of the other.

2. **When you are speaking, express your personal response** informed by your tradition, beliefs and practices as you have interpreted them in your life. Speak for yourself. Use 'I' language. Take ownership of what you say. Speak from your heart. Notice how often the phrases 'we all', 'of course', 'everyone says', 'you know' come into your conversation. The only person you can truly speak for is yourself.

3. **Listen without judgement.** The purpose of dialogue is to come to an understanding of the other, not to determine whether they are good, bad, right or wrong. If you are sitting there thinking, 'That's good,' 'That's bad,' 'I like that,' 'I don't like that,' you are having a conversation in your own mind, not listening to the speaker. Simply notice when you do this, and return to being present with the speaker.

4. **Suspend status.** Everyone is an equal partner in the enquiry. There is no seniority or hierarchy. All are colleagues with a mutual quest for insight and clarity. You are each an expert in your own life, and that's what you bring to the dialogue process.

5. **Honour confidentiality.** Leave the names of participants in the room so if you share stories or ideas, no one's identity will be revealed. Create a safe space for self-expression.

6. **Listen for understanding, not to agree with or believe.** You do not have to agree with or believe anything that is said. Your job is to listen for understanding.

7. **Ask clarifying or open-ended questions** to assist your understanding and to explore assumptions.

8. **Honour silence and time for reflection.** Notice what wants to be said rather than what you want to say.

9. **One person speaks at a time.** Pay attention to the flow of the conversation. Notice what patterns emerge from the group. Make sure that each person has an opportunity to speak, while knowing that no one is required to speak.

HOW THIS BOOK WAS CREATED
by Kay Lindahl

Writing and illustrating *The Sacred Art of Listening* was an interactive process. Each reflection was written after a process of inspiration, reflection and meditation. First, I asked myself the question 'What is the next topic?' before going into my practice of Centring Prayer. There was seldom an immediate answer.

Next, I asked the same question before I went for my morning run. Often several topics came to mind, and I allowed myself to explore each one. I let all of this percolate in my mind for a day or so. Then I sat down at my computer. I was amazed how readily the words came to me after this process of meditating and reflecting. Sometimes I let the draft sit for another day, reread it, and then decided what to leave in and what to add. Often, I used what was written in that first session. I believe that there was divine inspiration at work.

Writing the book was an exercise in inspired creativity – a marvellous learning experience. I listened for what wanted to be said from the spiritual practice of my experience as a listener and a listening teacher. I reflected on what had already been said, or on a recent life experience, or on something that was a particular concern. Above all, I wrote in the same way and using the same principles that I teach through my work in The Listening Center.

How the Art Was Created

by Amy Schnapper

As a supporter of the Alliance for Spiritual Community, I was familiar with Kay Lindahl's writing and, most important, with her voice. I was delighted when she asked me to create visual images to illuminate the text for the book she was writing.

A circle was selected as the unifying design element to reflect Kay's inspiration for the book, which she describes in 'The Circle of Life'. The circle's place in the mandalas of Eastern art and religion was not, consciously at least, the basis for the choice.

I found my own design inspiration in the titles of the reflections. I intentionally avoided reading the text of each reflection prior to doing the illustration, so I could trick my analytic mind into surrendering to inspiration. I created several series of five to seven illustrations each and, at the end of each series, matched the illustrations to the reflections that felt right to me. All of the illustrations were done by hand, not by computer. I like the feel of a pen in my hand and the focus required to create images in permanent black ink, which demands that all mistakes be embraced into the design. Like life itself, there are no mistakes – only lessons.

ACKNOWLEDGEMENTS

Living a life of gratitude is perhaps the best acknowledgement to everyone who has contributed to my spiritual growth and development over the years. I am deeply grateful for the opportunity to express their impact on my life with this book.

To Bishop Bob Anderson, my spiritual mentor and guide, whose gentle nudging opened my eyes to see what God was calling me to do and who consistently affirmed my progress.

To Steve Scholl and Joel Fotinos, whose early enthusiasm for the manuscript gave me moral support and encouraged me to keep moving forward.

To Jon Sweeney and the team at SkyLight Paths, who were such skilled and supportive midwives for the birth of this book.

To Amy Schnapper, who as artist was able to express my work with her unique art, who as partner demonstrates the ideal of harmonious collaboration, and who as friend is always there for me.

To Claire Nowland, our late partner, whose friendship transcends time and space. Her overwhelming response to this book can only be described as speechless enthusiasm!

To the participants and members of the many interfaith organisations that have played such an important role in my growth: the Alliance for

Spiritual Community, the Religious Diversity Faire, the Mastery Foundation, the North American Interfaith Network, the United Religions Initiative, and the Parliament of the World's Religions.

To my children and grandchildren, who warm my heart and inspire my soul with their cheers, hugs and kisses.

To my husband, life partner, best friend, who loves me for being me and in that space nurtures my full self-expression.

Thank you. I am truly blessed.

—Kay Lindahl

In my early forties when I began again being an artist, Bruce Nygren guided and mentored me, insisting on the same high standards for my creative work as he did for his own. Over the past decade, artist Bruce Bayard has embraced me in an enduring friendship, distinguished by his exceptional kindness and integrity. His guidance and direction helped bring this book into being.

—Amy Schnapper

Source Notes

Page 48: Don Miguel Ruiz, *The Four Agreements* (San Rafael, Calif.: Amber-Allen Publishing, 1997), vii.

Page 50: Hans Küng, *Global Responsibility: In Search of a New World Ethic,* trans. John Bowden (New York: Crossroad, 1991), 138.

Page 56: Henri J. M. Nouwen, *Reaching Out: The Three Movements of the Spiritual Life* (New York: Image Books, 1975), 136.

Page 80: Mother Teresa, *A Gift for God: Prayers and Meditations* (New York: Harper and Rowe, 1975), 68–69.

Page 89: Ernest Hemingway, as quoted in Larry Barker and Kittie Watson, *Listen Up* (New York: St. Martin's Press, 2000), xiii.

Page 90: Hafiz, *The Gift: Poems by the Great Sufi Master,* trans. Daniel Ladinsky (New York: Penguin Compass, 1999), 99.

Page 108: Frank Bianco, as quoted in Dale Salwak, *The Wonders of Solitude* (Novato, Calif.: New World Library, 1991), 56.

Page 112: Rainer Maria Rilke, *Letter to a Young Poet* (New York: Norton, 1954), 34–35.

Page 114, third paragraph: Margaret Mead, *Coming of Age in Samoa* (1928; New York: Harper Perennial, 2001).

Page 114, fourth paragraph: Deepak Chopra, *The Seven Spiritual Laws of Success* (San Rafael, Calif.: Amber-Allen Publishing, 1994), 70.

Page 124: Maha Ghosananda, personal communication with author, United Religions Initiative Global Summit, Stanford University, 1997.

Also from Wild Goose Publications:

PRAYING WITH OUR HANDS
21 practices of embodied prayer from
the world's spiritual traditions
Jon Sweeney

The power of words is nowhere more evident than when we use them to
pray, but prayer is also the place where we most often come up against the
limitations of words. In this intriguing book of reflections and accompany-
ing photographs, we see how our bodies, in particular our hands, can give
meaning to our prayers in a way that words alone cannot.

Here are twenty-one simple ways of using our hands to speak to God, presented in word and image. These spiritual practices are from a broad range
of religious traditions – from Anglican to Sufi, from Buddhist to Shaker.
Some may be familiar, some new; all demonstrate the universal importance
people of all faith traditions have given to embodied prayer. They teach us
to experience the unique spiritual enrichment that can be found when we
pray with our hands.

96pp · 1 901557 59 6 · £10.99 · 2001

Wild Goose Publications, the publishing house of the Iona Community established in the Celtic Christian tradition of St Columba, produces books, tapes and CDs on:

- holistic spirituality
- social justice
- political and peace issues
- healing
- innovative approaches to worship
- song in worship, including the work of the Wild Goose Resource Group
- material for meditation and reflection

If you would like to find out more about our books,
tapes and CDs, contact us at:

Wild Goose Publications
Fourth Floor, Savoy House
140 Sauchiehall Street,
Glasgow G2 3DH, UK

Tel. +44 (0)141 332 6292
Fax +44 (0)141 332 1090
e-mail: admin@ionabooks.com

or visit our website at
www.ionabooks.com
for details of all our products and online sales

WILD GOOSE PUBLICATIONS IS PART OF THE IONA COMMUNITY:

Founded in 1938 by the Revd George MacLeod, then a parish minister in Glasgow, this is an ecumenical Christian community committed to seeking new ways of living the Gospel in today's world. Initially working to restore part of the medieval abbey on Iona, the Community today remains committed to 'rebuilding the common life' through working for social and political change, striving for the renewal of the church with an ecumenical emphasis, and exploring new, more inclusive approaches to worship, all based on an integrated understanding of spirituality.

The Community now has over 240 Members, about 1500 Associate Members and around 1500 Friends. The Members – women and men from many denominations and backgrounds (lay and ordained), living throughout Britain with a few overseas – are committed to a fivefold Rule of devotional discipline, sharing and accounting for use of time and money, regular meeting, and action for justice and peace.

At the Community's three residential centres – the Abbey and the MacLeod Centre on Iona, and Camas Adventure Camp on the Ross of Mull – guests are welcomed from March to October and over Christmas. Hospitality is provided for over 110 people, along with a unique opportunity, usually through week-long programmes, to extend horizons and forge relationships through sharing an experience of the common life in worship, work, discussion and relaxation. The Community's shop on Iona, just outside the Abbey grounds, carries an attractive range of books and craft goods.

The Community's administrative headquarters are in Glasgow, which also serves as a base for its work with young people, the Wild Goose Resource Group working in the field of worship, a bi-monthly magazine, *Coracle*, and a publishing house, Wild Goose Publications.

For information on the Iona Community contact: The Iona Community, 4th Floor, Savoy House, 140 Sauchiehall Street, Glasgow G2 3DH, UK. Telephone: 0141 332 6343
e-mail: ionacomm@gla.iona.org.uk   web: www.iona.org.uk

For enquiries about visiting Iona, please contact: Iona Abbey, Isle of Iona, Argyll PA76 6SN, UK.
Telephone: 01681 700404   e-mail: ionacomm@iona.org.uk